HANDS UP

Dr. Janice Hutto Washington

Illustrated by Eric F. Quzack

Kingdom Builders Publications LLC

Second Edition 2018

DEDICATION

***HANDS UP** is dedicated to all parents, especially those of male children. This book is also dedicated to all caring adults with a heart to love our children, to teach our children, and to save our children. This book is sincerely dedicated to those children who have lost their lives by the hands of police officers.*

✻ ✻ ✻ ✻ ✻

PREFACE

Today, too many of our young people, especially African-American males are dying by the hands of police officers. There has been too much pain resonating through families, communities, and this nation. Our goal should be to eradicate this violence and bring our children home alive.

HANDS UP focuses on one strategy, and that's for parents and educators to teach children to come home alive. Our children need to be taught this strategy because a caring adult will not always be there to protect them.

It has become evident that police officers throughout this nation could benefit from more training. Let us not forget to train our children and the best place to begin is in the home. While nothing is guaranteed to be 100% safe, this book can render hope, faith, and greater efforts to bring our children home alive. **HANDS UP** can be a beginning!

THIS IS MY BOOK

Jason, you are my handsome and intelligent son who knows right from wrong. Mom loves you very much. Now Jason, my important question to you is, What would you do if you were stopped by the police? You are my only son and I want you to know that life, and some people, are not always fair.

You will be misjudged by your appearance. Your hair is in dread locks and just look at your clothes. You are wearing a hoodie and your pants are sagging. If you are ever stopped by the police, hold up your hands, fully open, to show that you do not wish to harm anyone. You want the police officers to know that you are a person of peace, not disruption.

Hold up your hands so negative thoughts won't enter the minds of the police officers. They will clearly see that there is nothing in your hands. You have no weapon! Be smart and stay alive! Hold up your hands!

Jason, hold up your hands and listen to every word that is spoken and be obedient to their commands. They will see this awesome child whom I gave life. Come home alive! I don't want to lose you. Hold up your hands!

Picture a time when you might be stopped by police officers and mommy won't be around. You need to know how to stay safe and alive. Keeping you safe is important to me because I want you to arrive home alive.

Jason, I love you and want you to return home. If you have on your hoodie, please remove it to show your strength. Please, my son, do not be afraid or fearful. Please think! Be smart! Use your head! Come home alive!

Jason, while the police officers are speaking, you silently pray this prayer in your mind and heart:

"Lord, keep me safe. Please help the police officers to see that I'm trying to do the right thing!"

Keep silent for you might say the wrong thing. Refrain from talking back because this might make the officers angry and nervous. Do not walk or run, just hold up your hands to try to get home alive.

Jason, if you are detained, continue to be silent. When time permits, call your family. Please stay positive regardless of the circumstances and believe that all will end well for you because you did the right thing.

Even when you are disrespected, stand firmly on what you've been taught. Remember, you want to come home alive.

Jason, be brave because you are a child of the King. Man cannot save you, so look to a higher power that is far greater than policemen, you, or even your mommy.

Jason, respecting others is NEVER wrong. It can have a great payoff!

Officer, thank you for bringing my Jason home safe and alive.

Jason, thank you so much for practicing self-control at all times. I am so proud of you!

Take the following poem with you as a reminder:

HANDS UP!
HANDS UP!
NOTHING IN THEM,
NOT EVEN A CUP.

HANDS UP!
LOOK AT ME,
I'M SOMEBODY'S CHILD!
BE KIND AND MILD.

HANDS UP!
JUST TELL ME WHAT TO DO.
TRYING TO COMPLY.
THE RULES YOU SUPPLY.

HANDS UP!
WILL SURRENDER AND SUBMIT!
NO JIVE!
LET ME MAKE IT HOME ALIVE.
HANDS UP! HANDS UP!

~ DR. JANICE HUTTO WASHINGTON

BIBLICAL REFERENCES

1 Chronicles 4:10

Isaiah 40:31

Proverbs 3:5-6

Exodus 14:14

1 Peter 2:9

Psalm 46:1

2 Timothy 1:7

1 Samuel 15:22

ABOUT THE AUTHOR

Janice Hutto Washington – a native of Denmark, South Carolina, is a published author, poet, lecturer, orator, educator, missionary, pastor, trailblazer, and humanitarian.

Dr. Washington has a strong passion for children, and has dedicated her life to impress upon children the seriousness of choice. Her first literary work, **HALF A RABBIT**, was aimed to build the confidence of children, and to plant seeds of hope. The success of the book has been globally recognized. **HANDS UP**, the second work, is written for all parents to influence their children on how to survive stressful encounters with hostile police officers.

www.ingramcontent.com/pod-product-compliance
Lightning Source LLC
Chambersburg PA
CBHW040734150426
42811CB00063B/1631